CHeCK IN
Being Present

Reach Out!

Learning to overcome negative thoughts and stay mindful is not the same as fighting depression. Do you feel overwhelmed by sadness? Remember, you matter. You are not alone. If you need help, reach out. Talk to an adult you love and trust. This could be a teacher, school counselor, or family member. Make an appointment with your doctor. Seek professional help. Or call the National Suicide Prevention Lifeline at 1-800-273-8255. Someone is available to talk with you 24 hours a day, every day.

45TH PARALLEL PRESS

Published in the United States of America by Cherry Lake Publishing
Ann Arbor, Michigan
www.cherrylakepublishing.com

Reading Adviser: Marla Conn, MS, Ed., Literacy specialist, Read-Ability, Inc.
Book Designer: Melinda Millward

Photo Credits: © SLP_London/Shutterstock.com, back cover, 12; © trofalenaRV/Shutterstock.com, cover, 5; © DreamStockIcons/Shutterstock.com, 6; © AaronAmat/istockphoto.com, 7; © Zakharova_Elena/Shutterstock.com, 8; © MAKSIM ANKUDA/Shutterstock.com, 10; © martin-dm/istockphoto.com, 11; © popicon/Shutterstock.com, 14; © noPPonPat/Shutterstock.com, 15; © Gordo25/Shutterstock.com, 16; © Andrija Nikolic/istockphoto.com, 17; © kuroksta/Shutterstock.com, 18; © Monkey Business Images/Shutterstock.com, 19; © LightField Studios/Shutterstock.com, 20; © Olkita/Shutterstock.com, 22; © PeopleImages/istockphoto.com, 23; © 4x6/istockphoto.com, 24; © musicman/Shutterstock.com, 26; © PamelaJoeMcFarlane/istockphoto.com, 27; © Syda Productions/Shutterstock.com, 28; © Mr.Cheangchai Noojuntuk/Shutterstock.com, 29; © Fotyma/Shutterstock.com, 30

Graphic Element Credits: © kkoman/Shutterstock.com, back cover, front cover, multiple interior pages; © str33tcat/Shutterstock.com, front cover, multiple interior pages; © NotionPic/Shutterstock.com, multiple interior pages; © CARACOLLA/Shutterstock.com, multiple interior pages; © VikiVector/Shutterstock.com, multiple interior pages

45th Parallel Press is an imprint of Cherry Lake Publishing.

Library of Congress Cataloging-in-Publication Data has been filed and is available at catalog.loc.gov

Printed in the United States of America
Corporate Graphics

Table of Contents

INtRODuCtiON

Have you ever felt out of control? Do you spend too much time thinking about the past? Do you spend too much time worrying about the future? Choose to live in the moment instead. Focus on the present. The present is a present. The present time is a gift.

Being present means being with your thoughts as they are. Don't push them away. Feel the experience of living your life. Check in and focus. Enjoy yourself. Focus on happy thoughts. This will make you happier and healthier.

This book gives you tips on how to be **mindful**. Mindful means being aware. It means taking care of your body and mind. Take a moment. Practice being present. Just breathe …

Tip: Choose to be present.

CHAPTER ONE
Take 3 Minutes to Breathe

You will experience different problems. You will have feelings about the problems. Then, you'll start thinking. Your thoughts could be **negative** or **positive**. Negative means bad. Positive means good.

Thinking is good. But overthinking, or too much thinking, can be bad. It can take you away from the present moment. You might feel trapped. You might lose awareness of what's going on. This will stop you from moving forward.

When this happens, take 3 minutes to breathe. Take a moment to center yourself. Start by slowing down. Take a few deep breaths. Step away from thinking. Bring yourself to the present moment.

· · · · · · · · · ▶ **Tip**: Schedule time in your day to do mindful breathing. Set an alarm to remind yourself. Do this until it becomes a habit.

In the first minute, ask yourself these questions:

- Where am I?
- What is around me?
- What am I feeling?

In the second minute, direct attention away from your thoughts. Focus on something in the present moment. This can be a leaf on the ground. It can be a person you're with. It can be a pen.

In the third minute, focus on your breath. Try to forget everything else. Take a deep breath. Follow your breath as it enters and exits your body. Do this as many times as you need to.

· · · · · · ➤ **Tip**: Put some glitter in a jar. Add water. Shake it up. Focus on the glitter. Watch as tiny, shiny pieces fall to the bottom.

Science Connection

Dr. Matthew A. Killingsworth studies human happiness. He's a psychologist. He studied at Harvard University. He said people spend nearly 47 percent of their waking hours thinking about things other than what they're doing. This means people are not in the present. Killingsworth said, "People are substantially less happy when their minds are wandering than when they're not ... If we learn to fully engage in the present, we may be able to cope more effectively with the bad moments and draw even more enjoyment from the good ones." Humans can focus attention on other things than the present. No other living thing can do this. Animals focus on surviving. They focus on the present. Humans are special. Our minds wander a lot. When our minds wander, we often think about bad things. We may think about worries and fears. This causes unhappiness. This is why it's important to form a habit of positive thinking.

CHAPTER TWO
Do a
Body Scan

Our lives can get so busy. We can get lost in all the fuss. It's important to stay in tune with your body. Doing a body **scan** is a great way to start your day. A scan is an inspection. A body scan is like a body check.

You can do this standing, sitting, or lying down. Just be comfortable. Start by taking deep breaths. Keep doing this until you feel calm and relaxed. (But don't fall asleep!)

Focus on 1 body part at a time. Start with your toes. Think about how your toes feel. Wiggle them. Stretch them out. Curl them back in.

Tip: Pretend that you're on a tiny boat. Imagine yourself traveling to all parts of your body.

From your toes, move on to your feet. Next are the ankles and legs. Continue focusing on 1 body part at a time as you travel up your body to the top of your head. Feel the heaviness of each body part. Think about the **sensations**. Sensations are feelings related to senses. Move each body part. Feel gravity pushing down as you move. Feel the air surrounding that body part.

You can also do a body scan while walking. Focus on the sensations of walking. Feel the small and large movements. Focus on the swish of your arms. Pay attention each time your shoe hits the pavement.

Tip: Play music. Move to the music. Move 1 body part at a time. Start by tapping your feet. Then, roll your shoulders or wiggle your hips. Feel each motion.

Real-Life Scenarios

Life is full of adventures. There will be challenges. Things happen. Make good choices. These are some events you could face:

- You're studying for a test. Instead of reading your notes, your mind wanders. You worry about failing. Why is this not productive? How can you focus more on the present?

- Your mother gives you a long list of chores. You can't hang out with friends until they're done. How do you feel? What can you do to get started?

- You run into an old friend. You remember that your last meeting didn't end well. You get upset thinking about the past. How do you bring yourself back to the present? How is your present self different from your past self? How can you respond to your friend with your present self?

CHAPTER THREE
Savor the Moment

To **savor** means to taste and enjoy completely. When people savor the moment, they appreciate being alive.

Each day, choose a different moment to savor. Focus on things that you'd usually rush through. For example, these could be your goals for the first week:

- Sunday: Brushing your teeth
- Monday: Making the bed
- Tuesday: Taking a shower
- Wednesday: Washing dishes
- Thursday: Doing homework
- Friday: Eating a meal
- Saturday: Putting away laundry

Tip: Eat your favorite thing. Enjoy every second of it. Think of nothing else.

For each task, do it slowly. Don't hurry. Don't focus on getting done. Instead, focus on what you're doing. Don't think about anything else. Push all other thoughts out of your head. Also, take a few minutes to be grateful. For example, think about how easy it is for you to grab a glass of clean water.

You can also add new tasks to your day. An example is the act of making a cup of tea. Be deliberate with how you make it. Or try doing something new. Go for a walk around the neighborhood. Do it in peace. Do it without **distractions**. Distractions are things that can take you away from your goals. Bring your phone with you, but put it on silent.

Live in the present. Don't focus on the past or future. Find joy in living every moment.

Tip: Make a list. Do 1 thing at a time. Don't move on until you've finished something completely.

CHAPTER FOUR
Go Backward

Sometimes, we lose track of time. We're so busy working that we forget about everything else. How can we live in the moment if we're not aware of the present? Time moves on. We don't get it back. Be mindful of each moment. Don't get too comfortable with habits and routines. We need to be **flexible**. Flexible means able to make changes.

Try to **reverse** the order you do things. Reverse means to go backward. For example, think about how you dress yourself. If you put your pants on first, put your shirt on first instead.

Tip: Take a different route to school. Explore new paths. Take note of your surroundings.

Doing things in reverse will make you more aware of the things you're doing. It'll break you out of your routines. This will help you be more flexible. Making plans is good. But it's also important to go with the flow. Go where the moment takes you!

Another challenge is to use your **opposite** hand. Opposite refers to the other side of something. For example, if you brush your hair with your right hand, use your left hand instead. This will make you pay more attention to what you're doing.

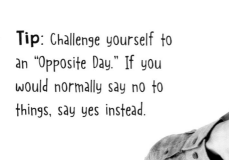

Tip: Challenge yourself to an "Opposite Day." If you would normally say no to things, say yes instead.

Spotlight Biography

Thich Nhat Hanh said, "Drink your tea . . . slowly, evenly, without rushing toward the future." Hanh was born in 1926. He's a Vietnamese Buddhist monk. He's a peace activist. He's a poet. He's written over 100 books. He travels around the world. He gives many speeches. He talks about being present. He talks about being peaceful. His key teaching is that, through mindfulness, we can learn to live happily in the present moment. He thinks being present is the only way to develop peace in one's self and in the world. He helped make Buddhism popular in the United States and Europe. He founded 6 monasteries. A monastery is a community of monks. Hanh is the leader of over 700 monks and nuns all over the world. He has also inspired over 1,000 sanghas. Sanghas are local mindfulness practice communities.

CHAPTER Five
Experience All 5 Senses

We have 5 senses. The senses are sight, touch, hearing, smell, and taste. We use our eyes to see. We use our hands to touch. We use our ears to hear. We use our nose to smell. We use our mouths and tongues to taste.

Our senses help us experience things fully. They're working all the time. Sometimes we forget about them.

This next activity focuses on each of our senses. It makes us aware of each sense. It makes us aware of our surroundings. It makes us more present.

Tip: Find a place with a view. Maybe sit by a window. Or go to a park. Sit on a bench. Engage all 5 of your senses.

You can do this activity anywhere. All you have to do is look around you. Do the following:

- Find 5 things you can see. Pick things that you wouldn't normally notice.
- Find 4 things you can feel. Notice the different **textures**. Textures are the ways surfaces feel.
- Find 3 things you can hear. Listen for sounds. Try to separate each sound. Focus on one sound at a time. Push the other sounds out of your mind.
- Find 2 things you can smell. Note if the smells are good or bad. Describe the smells.
- Find 1 thing you can taste. Note if it tastes good or bad. Describe the taste.

Tip: Walk around in a dark room or blindfolded. Use your other senses to figure out what things are.

Fun Fact

Being present also means showing up. Some students have perfect attendance. This means they didn't miss any school days. They went to school every single day. Some schools give out special awards for having perfect attendance from kindergarten through grade 12. For example, a high school in Arizona gave away a car. An elementary school in Kentucky gave away bikes. Many schools host pizza parties. Zhariah Walker took perfect attendance to the extreme. Walker went to school in South Carolina. She's the third member of her family to have 12 years of perfect attendance. Her mother and her brother also earned perfect attendance. Walker said, "The bar was set high, and I was determined to reach it." Walker had at least a 3.5 GPA. She got accepted into over 60 colleges. She wants to study business and law.

CHAPTER SIX
Take a Vacation Day

Vacations are breaks or holidays. They're time away from our regular lives. People relax on vacations. Many people go to different places for their vacations. They take trips.

You don't have to go far to have a vacation. If you're present, every day can be a vacation. Choose a different vacation every day. Here are some ideas:

- Go on a walk. Explore a new area of town.
- Go on a picnic with a friend.
- Take a hot bath. Add bubbles for more fun.
- Watch the sunrise. Or watch the sunset.
- Read a book. Or listen to a book while walking.

Tip: Take a trip in nature. Be outside. Take note of the natural beauty. Breathe in fresh air.

This is your time to be calm. Set aside your worries and fears. Experience what is happening. Take in all the sights and sounds. Engage your senses. Be aware of what's happening around you. Be aware of what's happening within you.

Take a break. Take time to **recharge**. Recharge means to rest and get new energy. Our minds and bodies need rest.

Challenge yourself to be tech-free. Spend time away from your **devices**. Devices are things like phones. Disconnect from technology. Instead, connect with yourself. Connect with nature. Connect with other people.

Tip: While on vacation, focus more on the experience than on taking pictures. See with your eyes, not your camera.

HOST YOUR OWN MINDFULNESS EVENT!

Feeling unfocused? Is your mind wandering? Are you thinking too much about the past or future? This might be the best time to host your own mindfulness event! Celebrate the present moment. Host a "Be Present" Party!

STEP ONE: Figure out where you can host your party.

STEP TWO: Make invitations—and get creative! Ask a friend to help you. Send out the invitations.

STEP THREE: Plan your activities and get supplies.

Mind Messages!

- Give everyone a blank piece of paper. Give everyone a pen or pencil.

- Tell everyone to write down all their "mind chatter." Mind chatter is thoughts and ideas in one's head. It tends to be random. It tends to be distracting. It tends to be all over the place.

- Encourage people to write anything and everything that's on their mind. Tell them no one will read this. There is no wrong way to do this.

- After 10 minutes, tell people to rip up the paper into tiny pieces. Say, "Let your mind chatter sit on the page. Clear your mind. Now, focus on being present."

Minding the Mindfulness Cue!

- Give everyone a piece of string.

- Set out beads and charms.

- Make bracelets. Add the beads and charms. Be creative.

- Tell people that they made a "mindfulness cue." Say, "Sometimes, it's hard to remember to be mindful. We get busy. We get overwhelmed. When this happens, look at your bracelet. This should remind you to be mindful."

Mindful Review!

- Sit in a circle. Cross your legs. Keep your backs straight. Close your eyes.

- Lead others in a mindful review of the day. Say the following prompts one at a time. After each prompt, give people 2 minutes to think.

  - Think back to the start of the day.

  - Think through the rest of your day.

  - Find a memorable moment.

  - Focus on that moment.

  - How did you feel?

  - Focus on this moment.

  - How do you feel right now?

- Give people paper and crayons. Have them create a color that describes their mood. Encourage people to do this every day and to keep track of their colors.

GLOSSARY

devices (dih-VISE-iz) tools that connect to technology like phones, tablets, and televisions

distractions (dih-STRAKT-shuhnz) things that can take you away from your goals

flexible (FLEK-suh-buhl) having the ability to make changes or go with the flow

mindful (MINDE-ful) focusing one's awareness on the present moment to center the mind, body, and soul

negative (NEG-uh-tiv) thoughts and feelings that evoke sadness, anger, fear, or general unhappiness

opposite (AH-puh-zit) the other side of something

positive (PAH-zih-tiv) thoughts and feelings that evoke happiness

recharge (ree-CHARJ) to gain new energy after resting

reverse (rih-VURS) to go backward, to change the order

savor (SAY-vur) to taste and enjoy completely

scan (SKAN) inspection, check

sensations (sen-SAY-shuhz) feelings related to senses

textures (TEKS-churz) the ways that surfaces feel, such as rough or smooth

vacations (vay-KAY-shuhnz) breaks or holidays used for rest and relaxation

INDEX

ABOUT THE AUTHOR

Dr. Virginia Loh-Hagan is an author, university professor, and former classroom teacher. This book made her think about Doris Day's version of the song "Enjoy Yourself." She lives in San Diego with her very tall husband and very naughty dogs. To learn more about her, visit www.virginialoh.com.